Rose Coloring Book

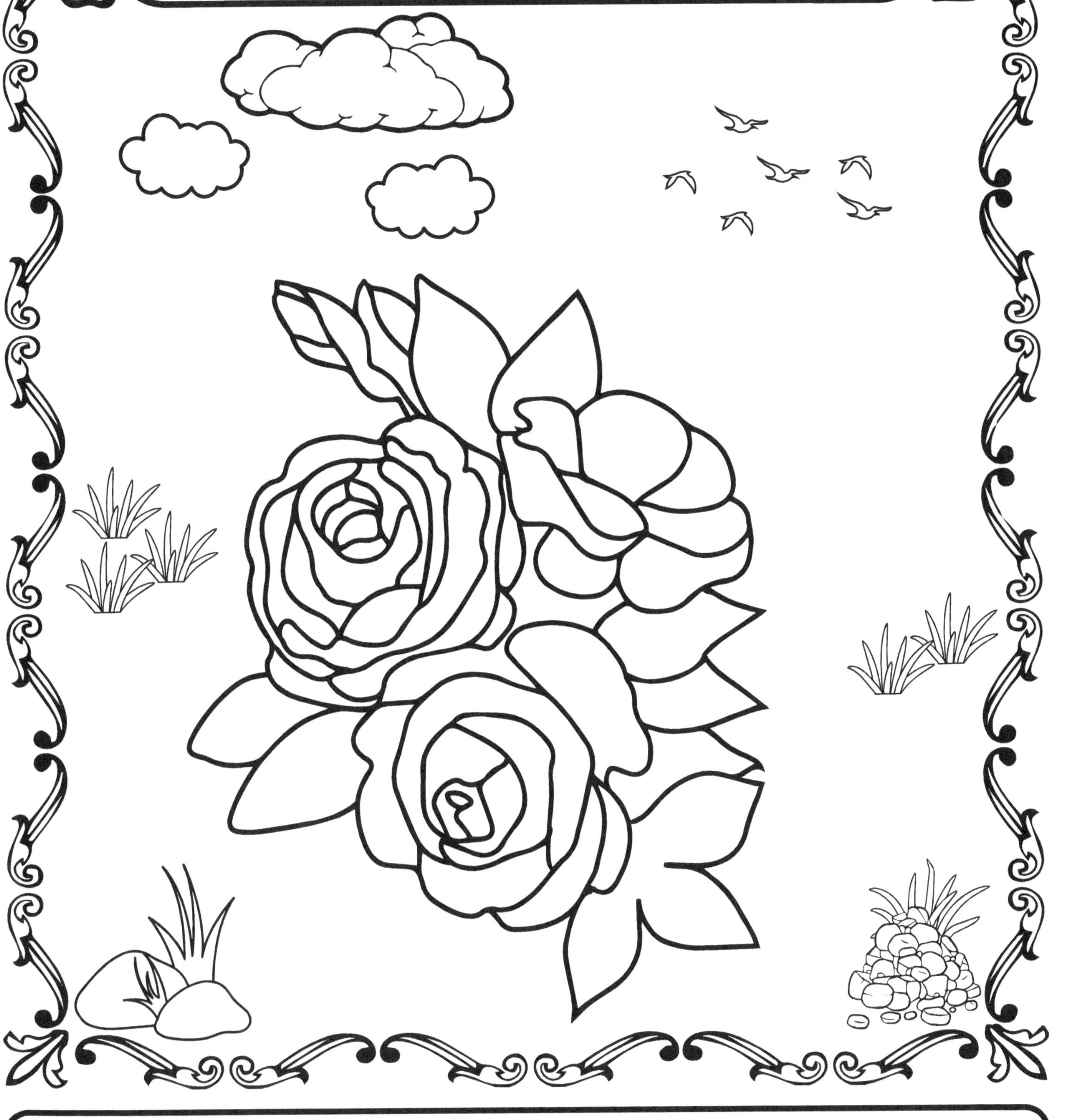

Rose Coloring Book

Rose Coloring Book

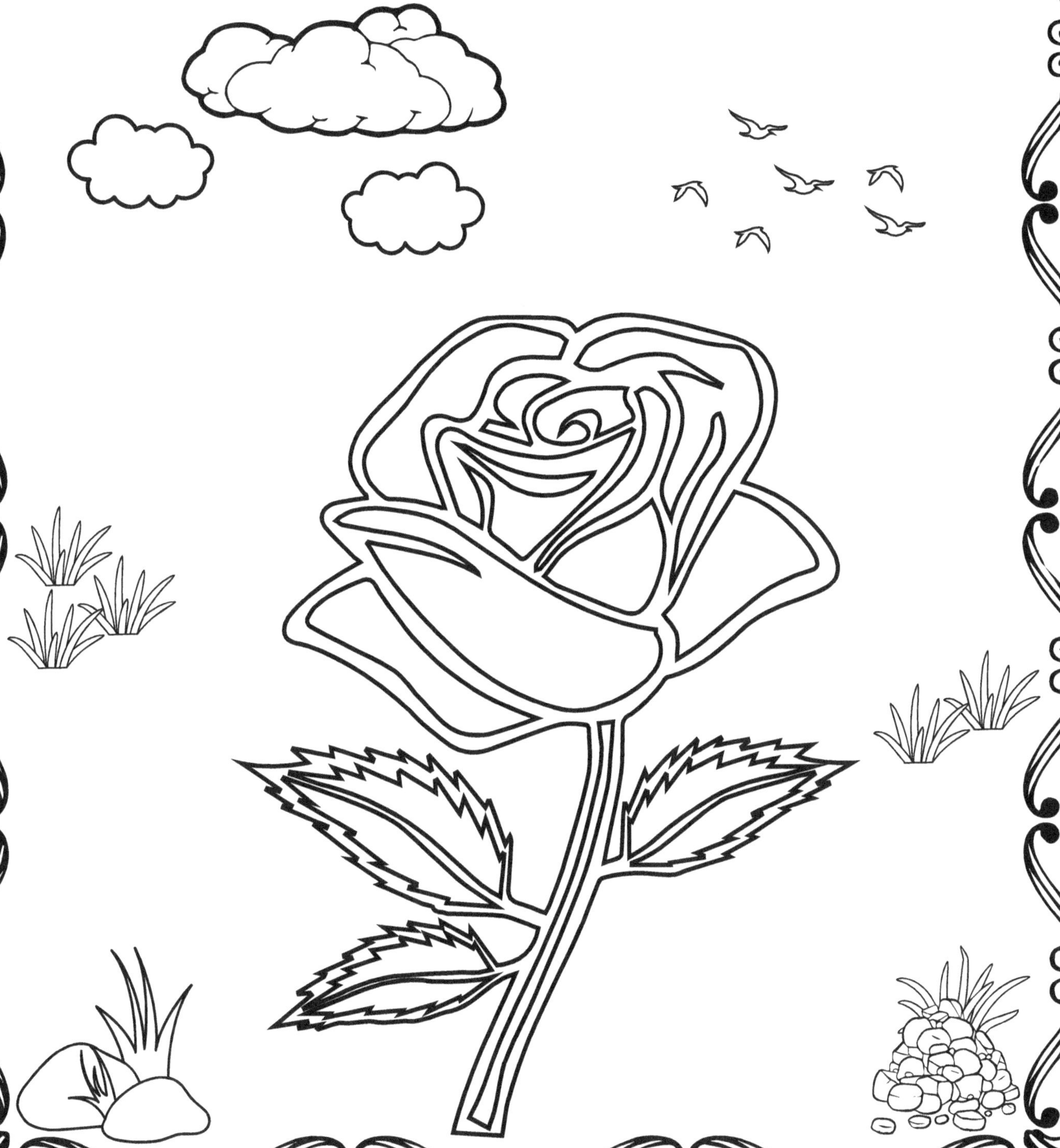

Rose Coloring Book

Rose Coloring Book

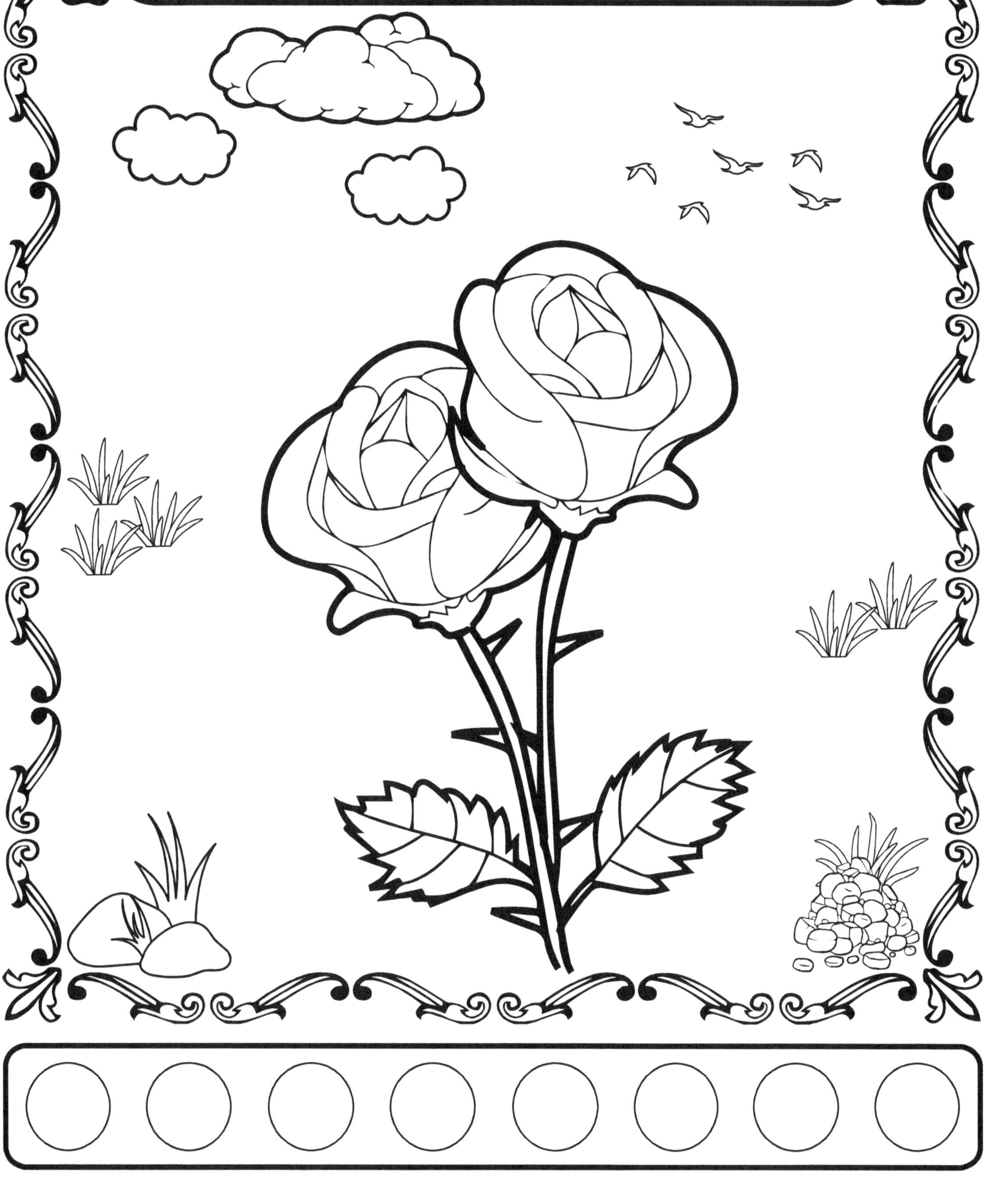

Rose Coloring Book

Rose Coloring Book

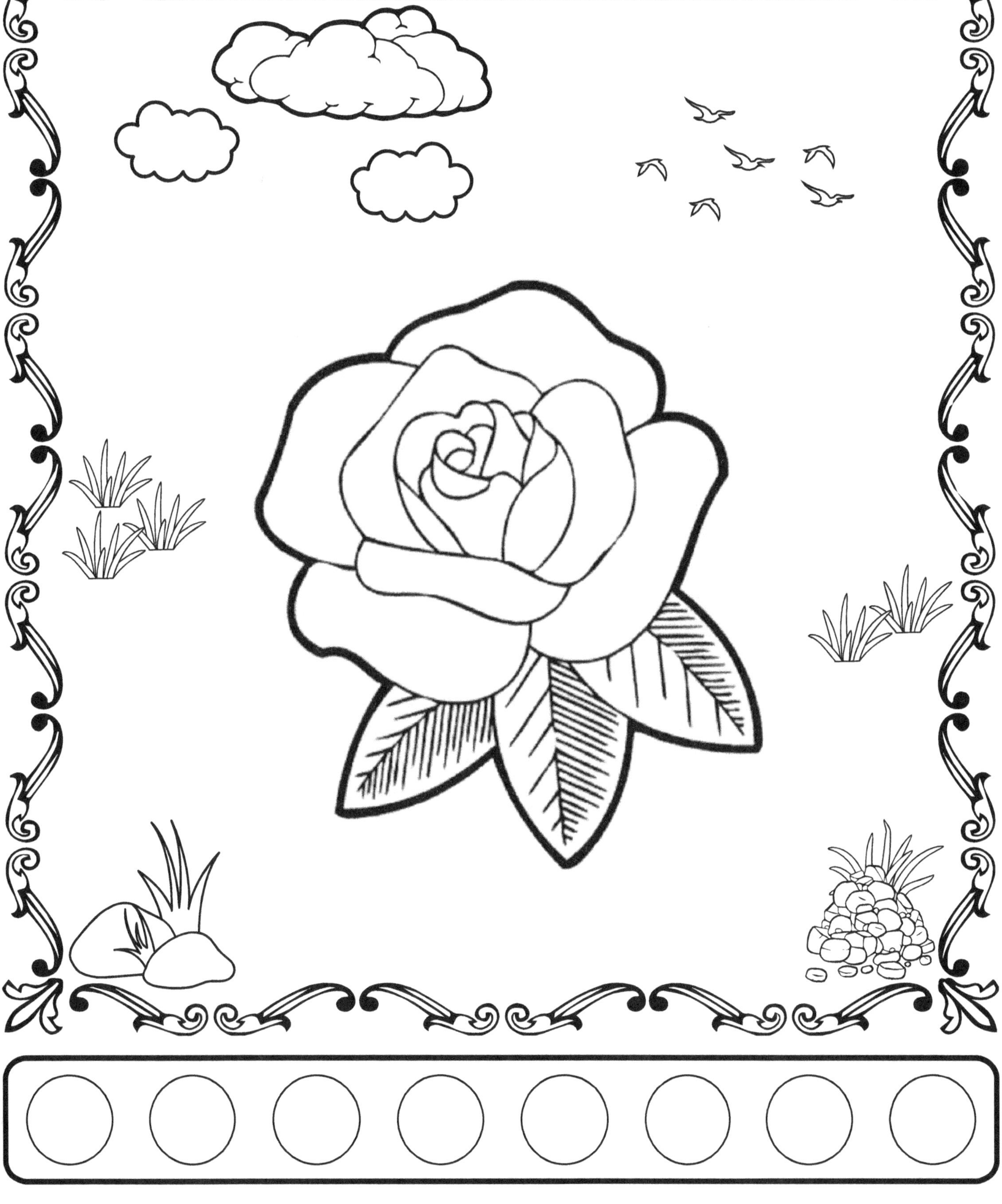

Rose Coloring Book

Rose Coloring Book

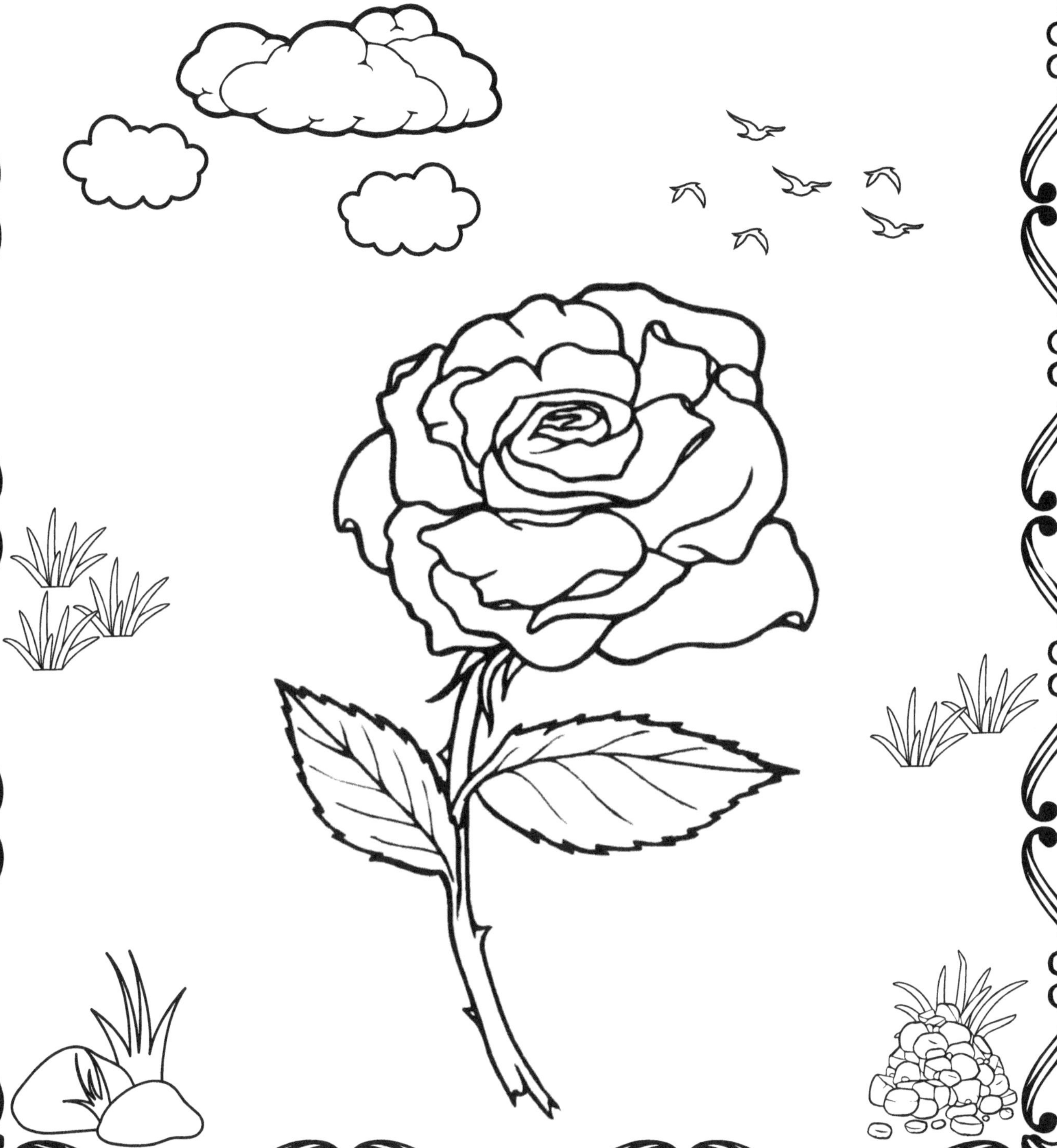

Rose Coloring Book

Rose Coloring Book

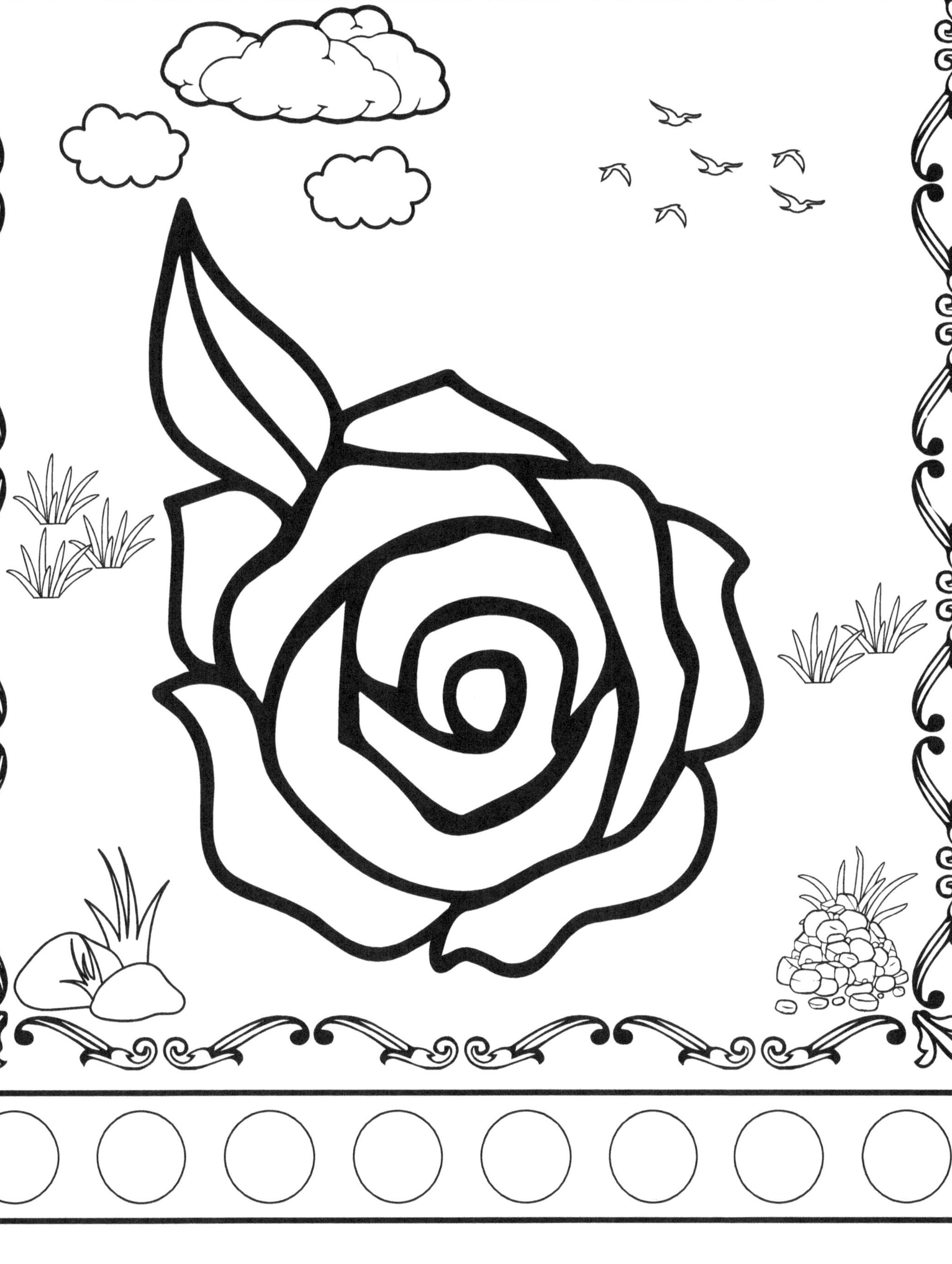

Rose Coloring Book

Rose Coloring Book

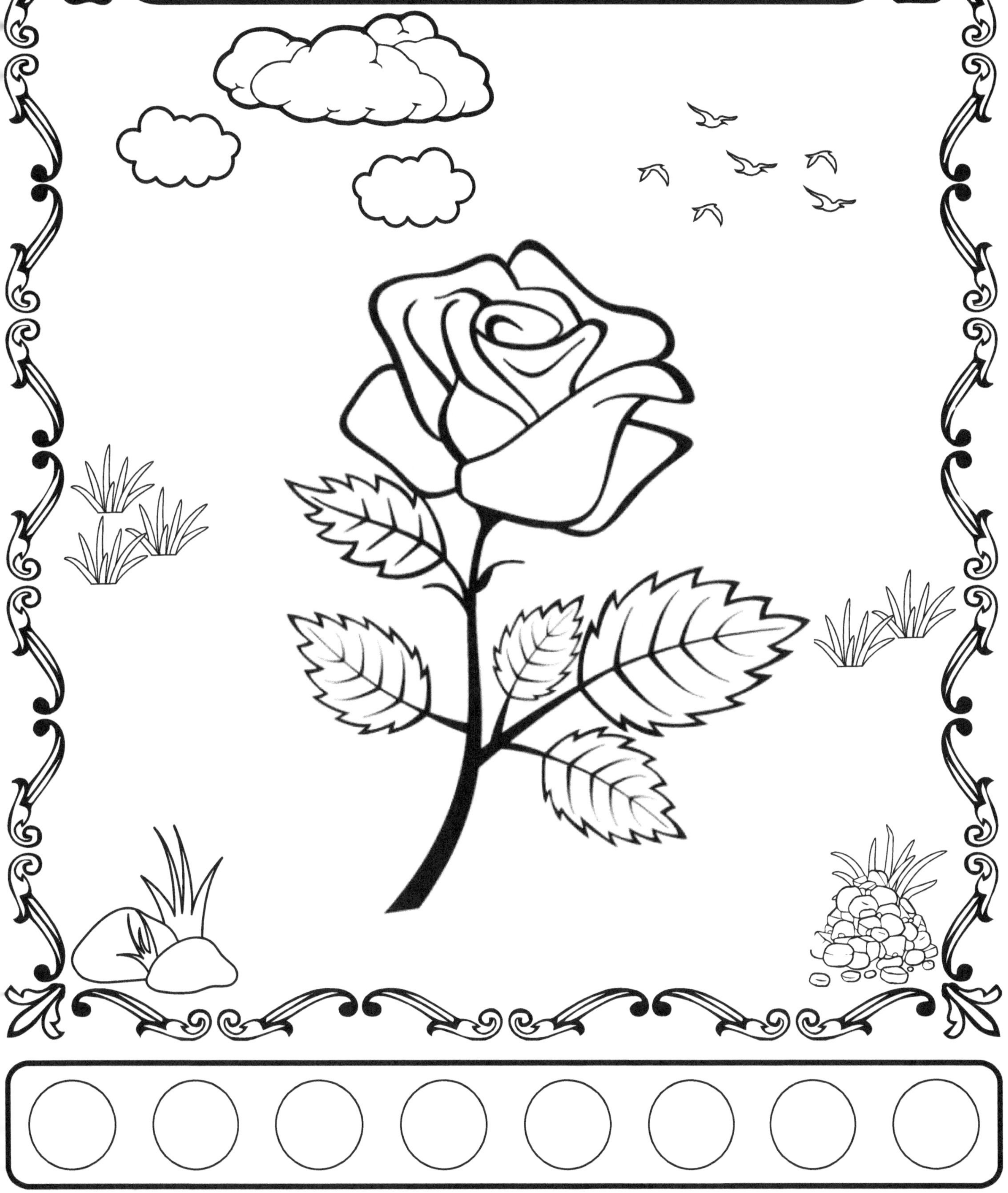

Rose Coloring Book

Rose Coloring Book

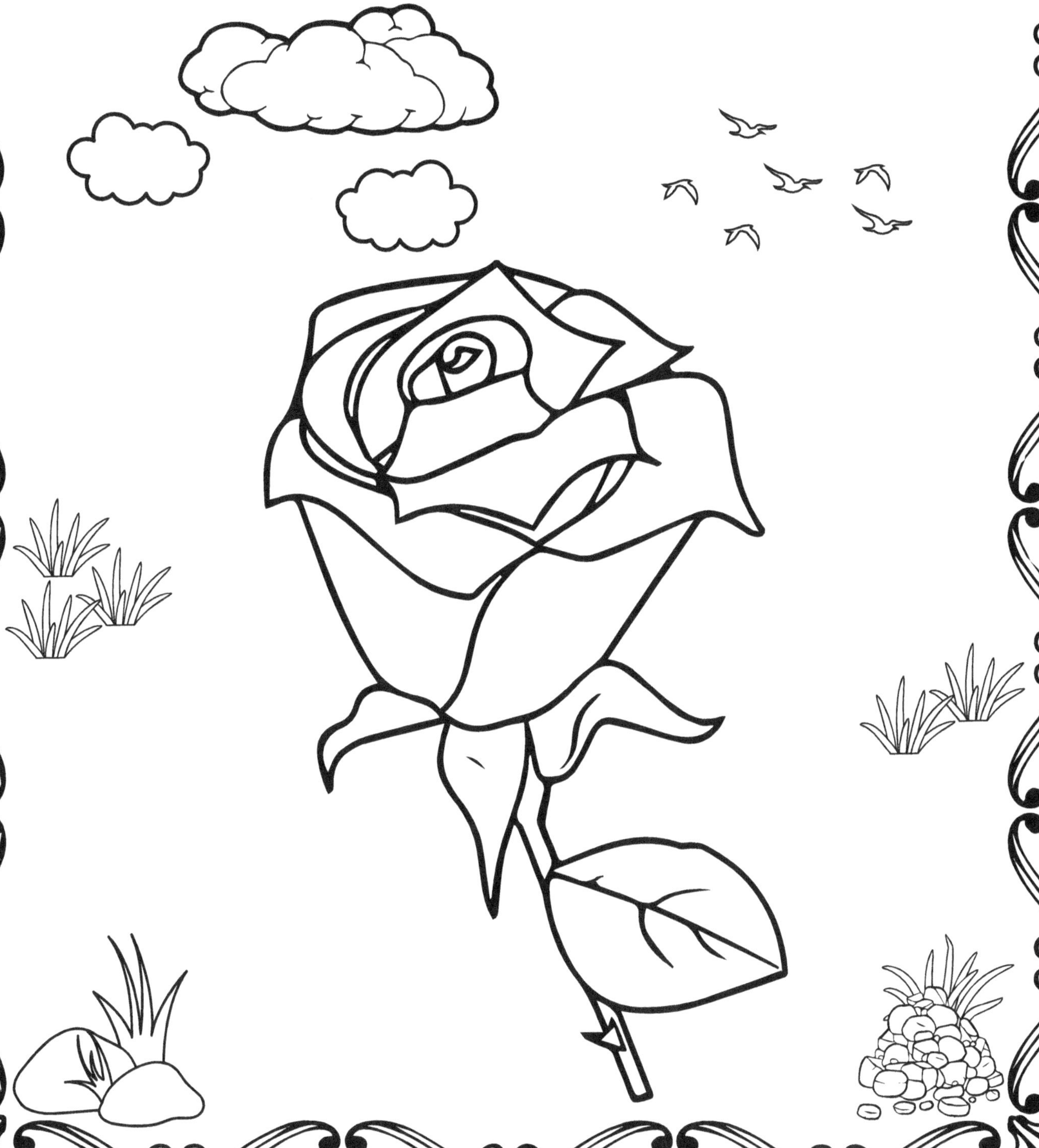

Rose Coloring Book

Rose Coloring Book

Rose Coloring Book

Rose Coloring Book

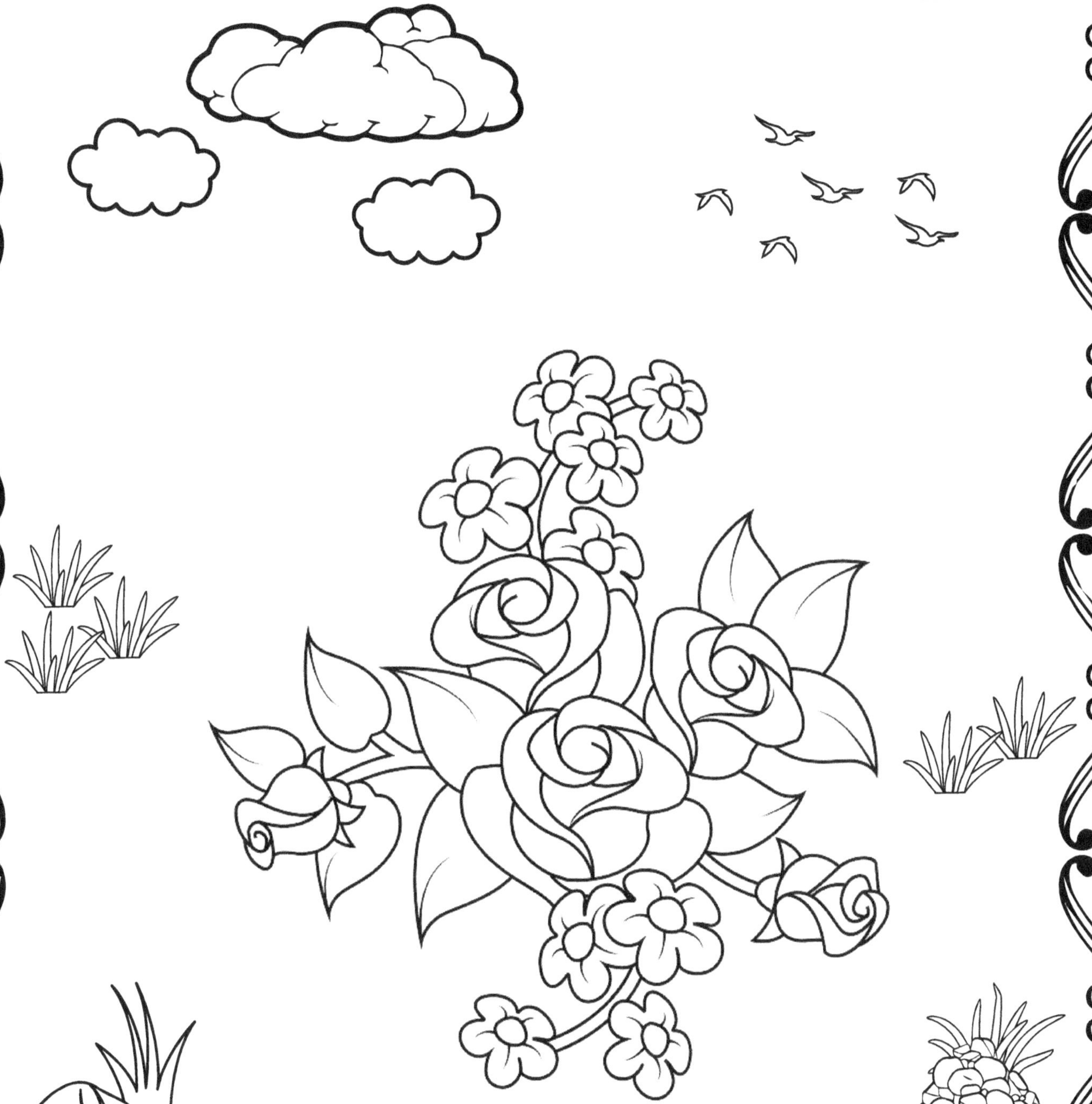

Rose Coloring Book

Rose Coloring Book

Rose Coloring Book

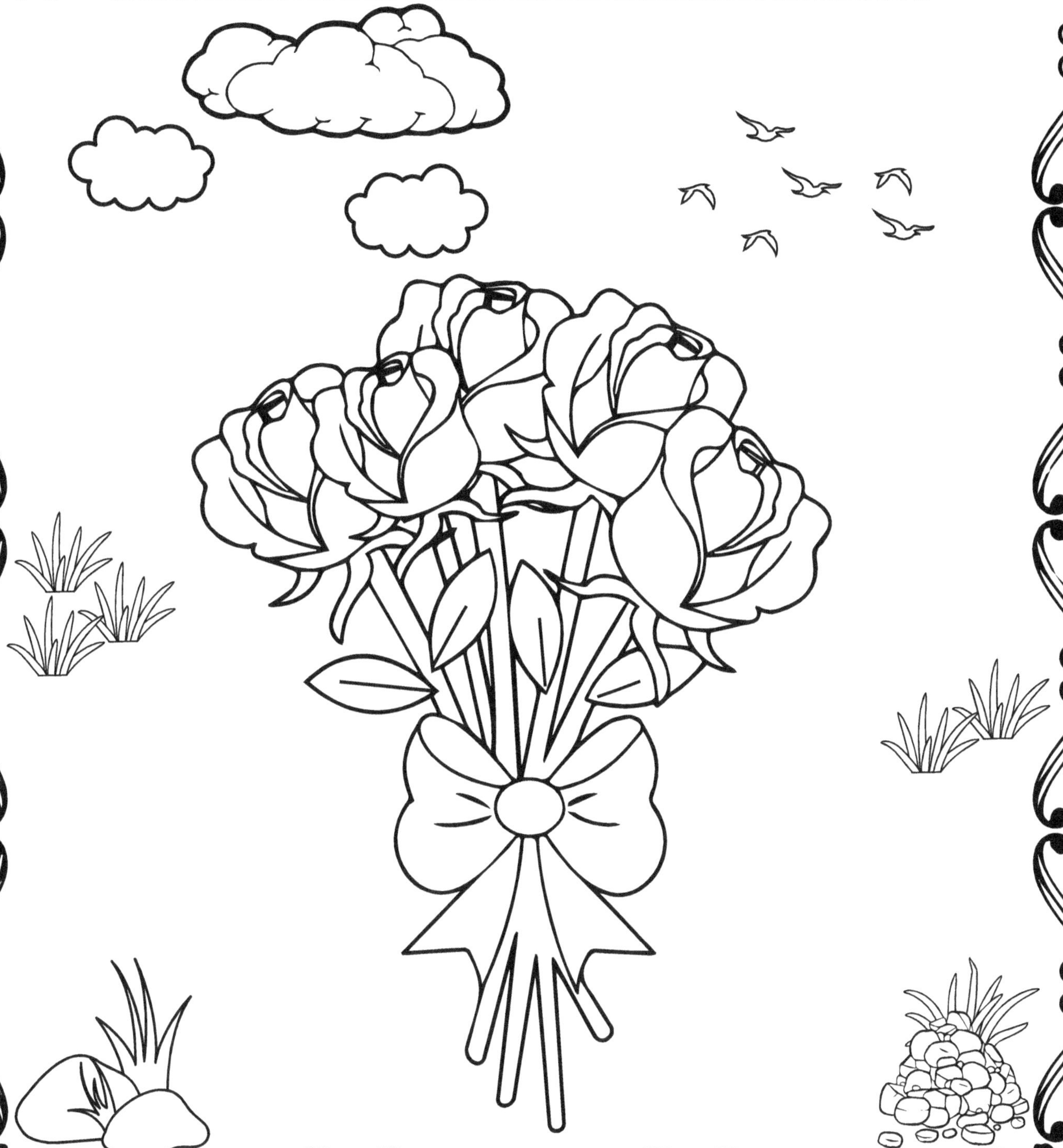

Rose Coloring Book

Rose Coloring Book

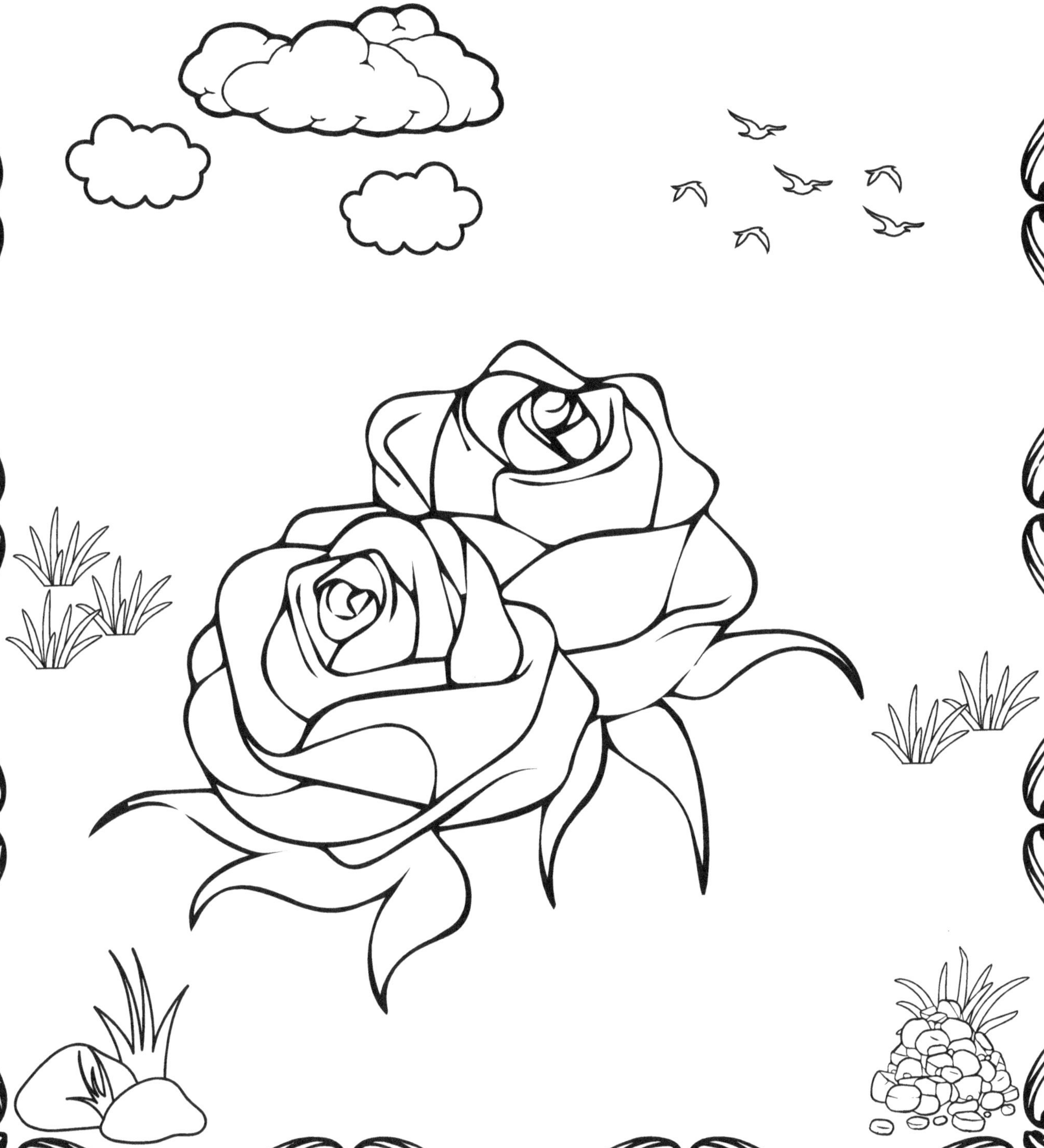

Rose Coloring Book

Rose Coloring Book

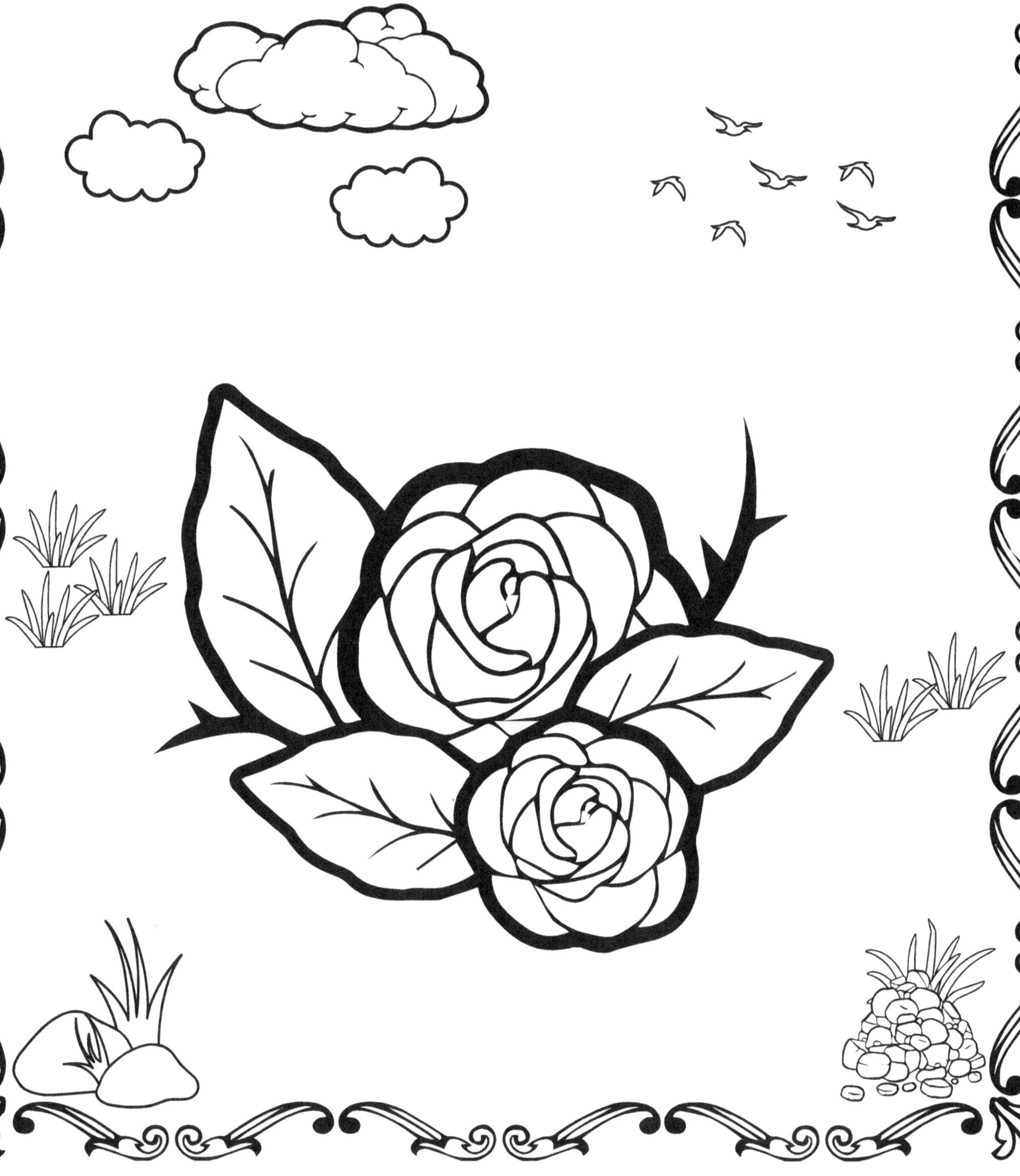

Rose Coloring Book

Rose Coloring Book

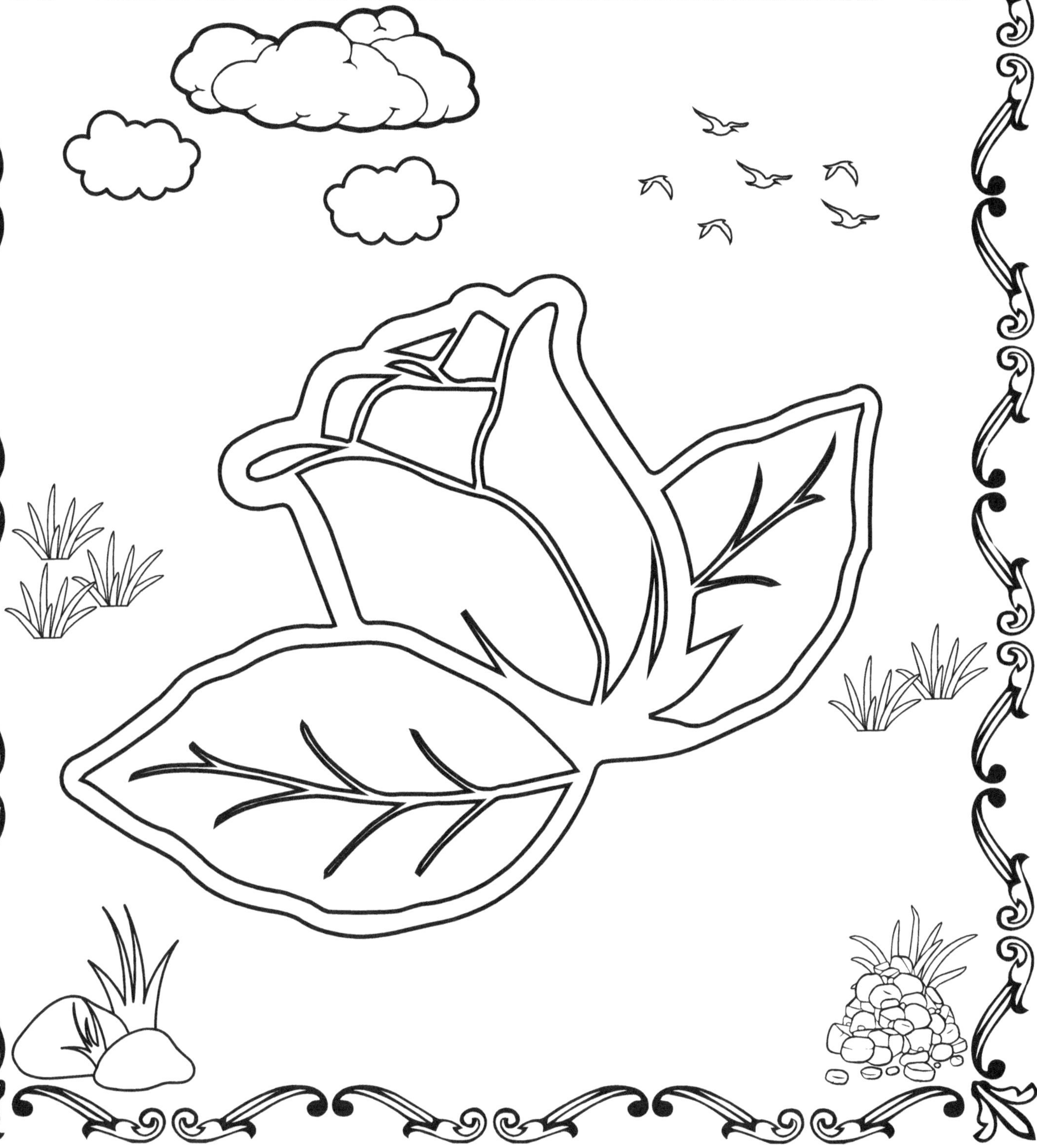

Rose Coloring Book

Rose Coloring Book

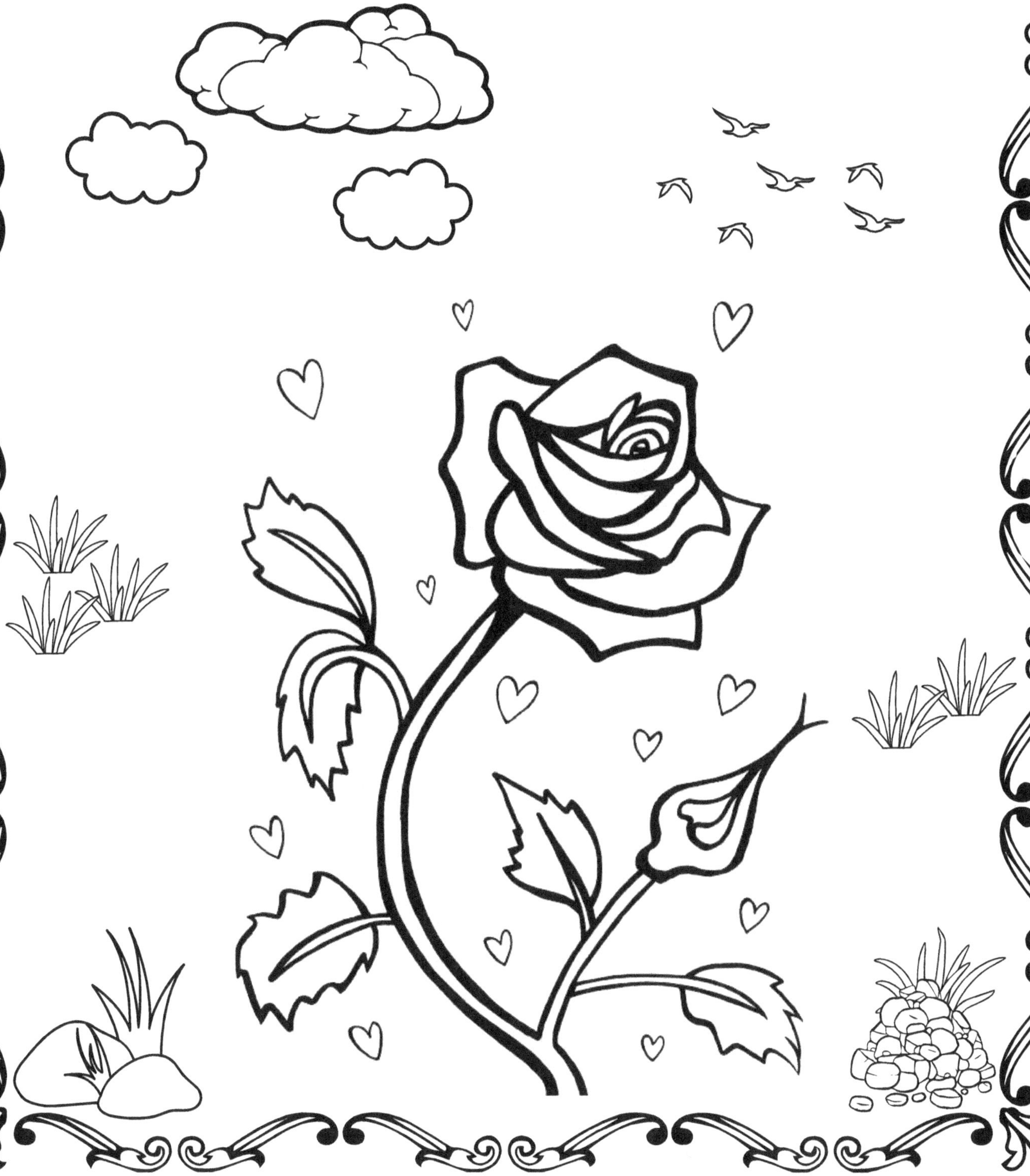

Rose Coloring Book

Rose Coloring Book

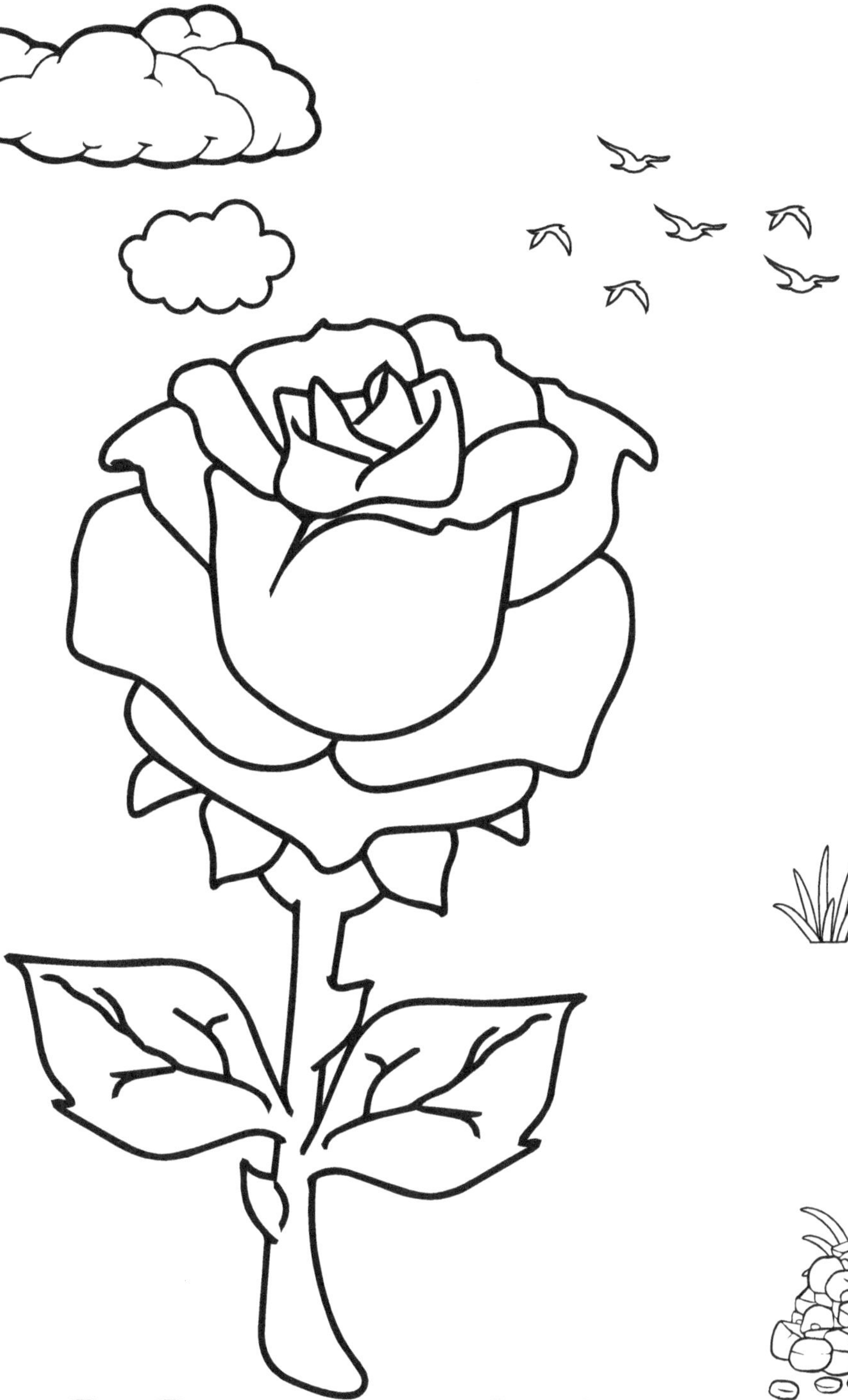

Rose Coloring Book

Rose Coloring Book

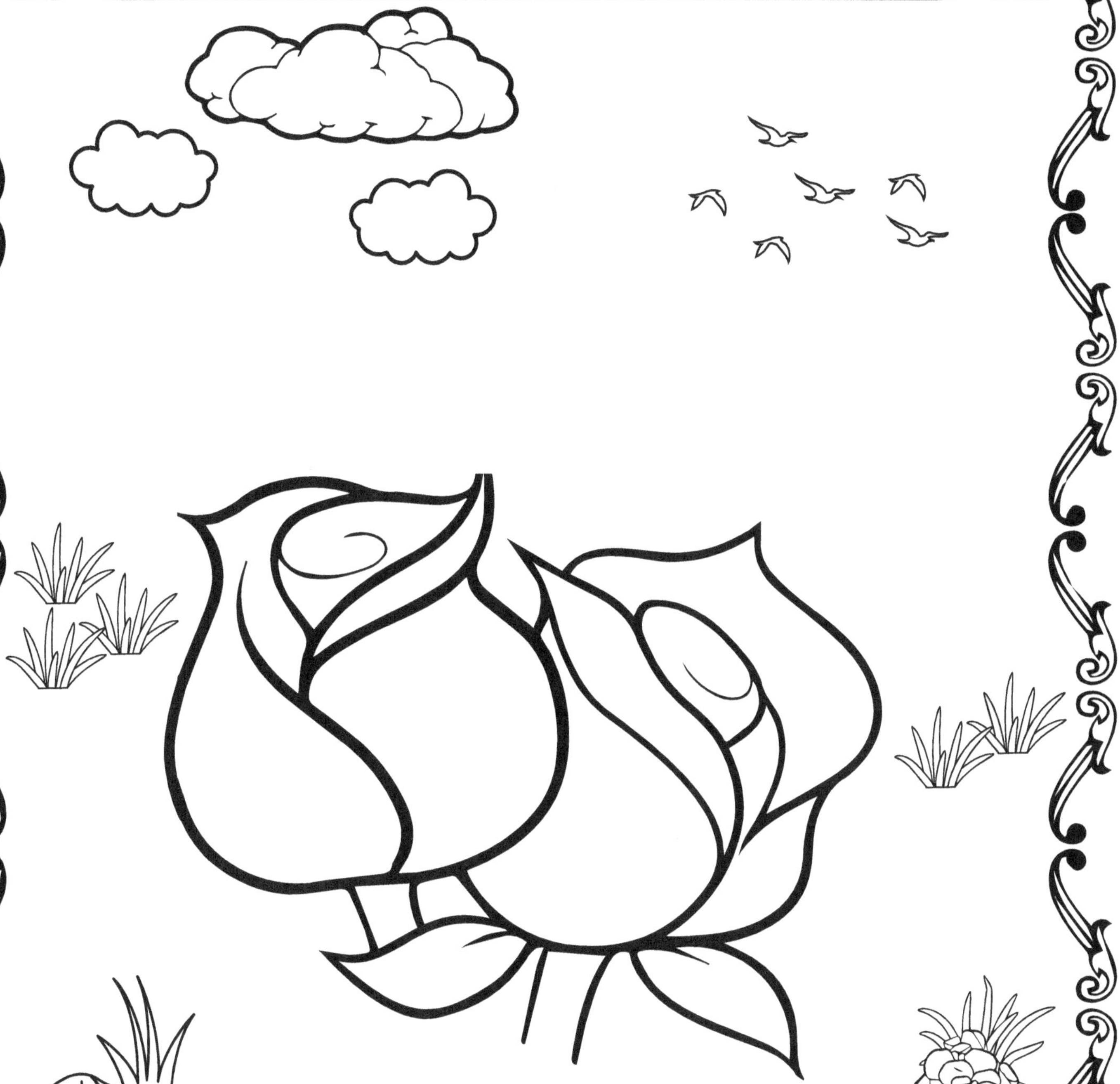

Rose Coloring Book

Rose Coloring Book

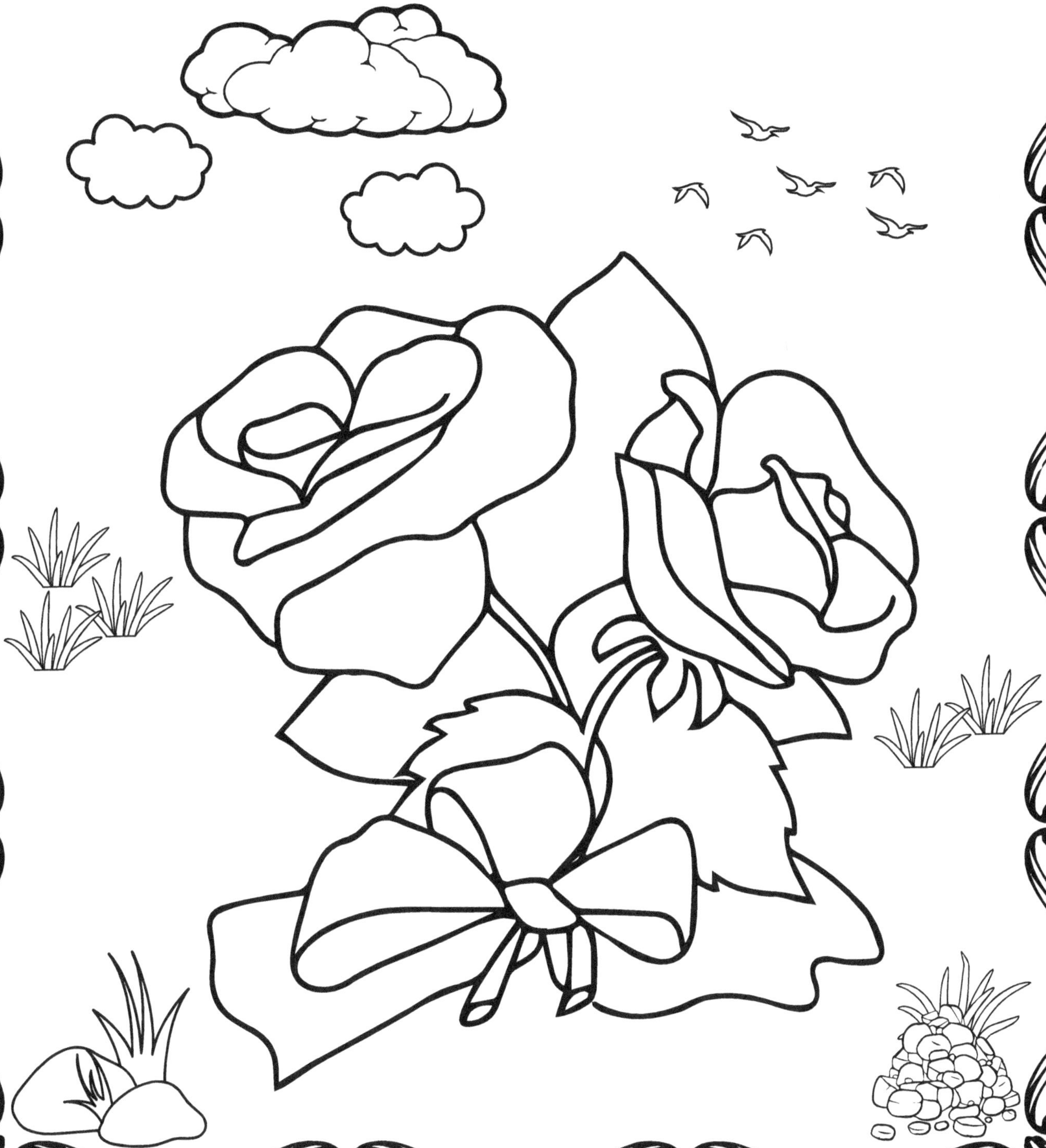

Rose Coloring Book

Rose Coloring Book

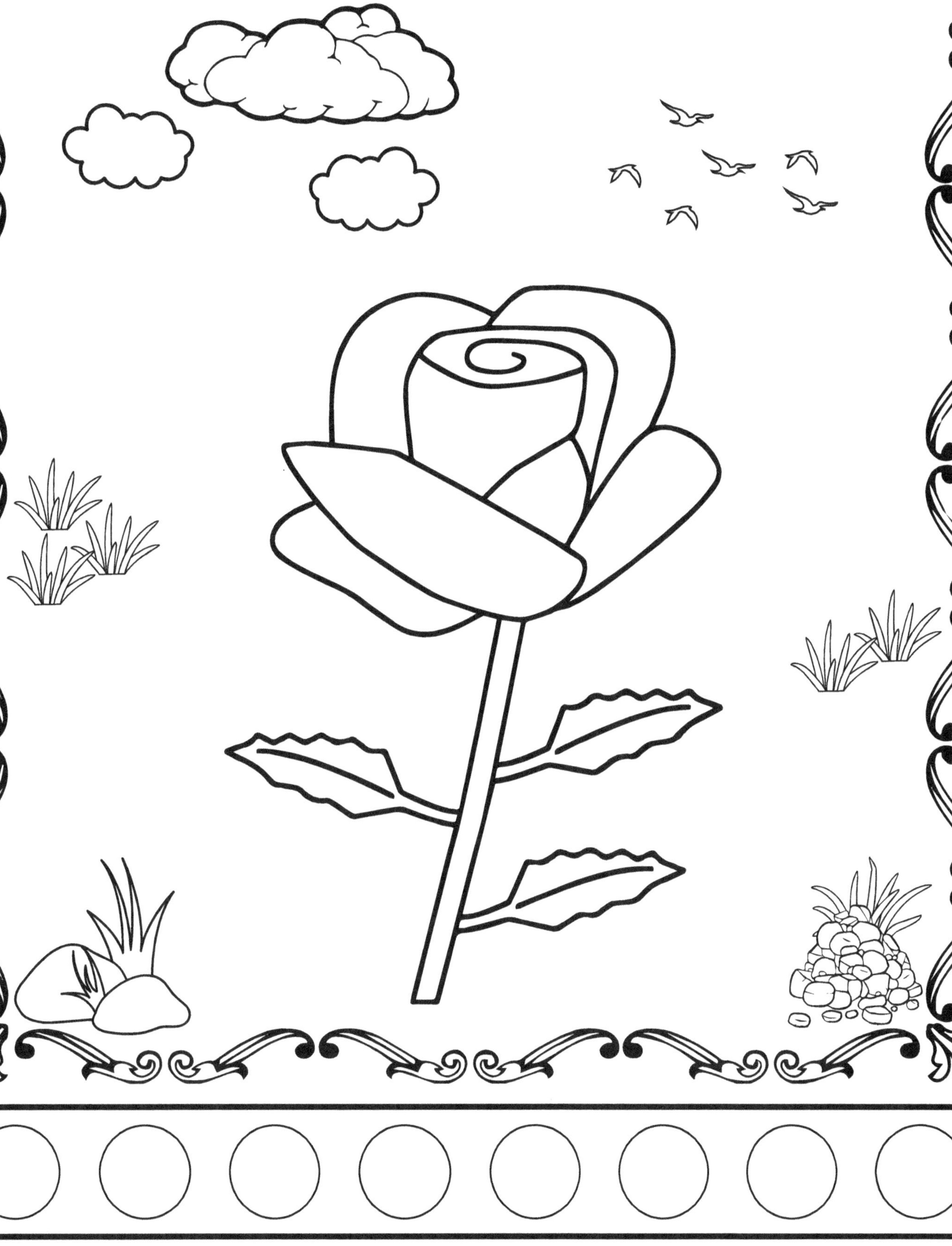

Rose Coloring Book

Rose Coloring Book

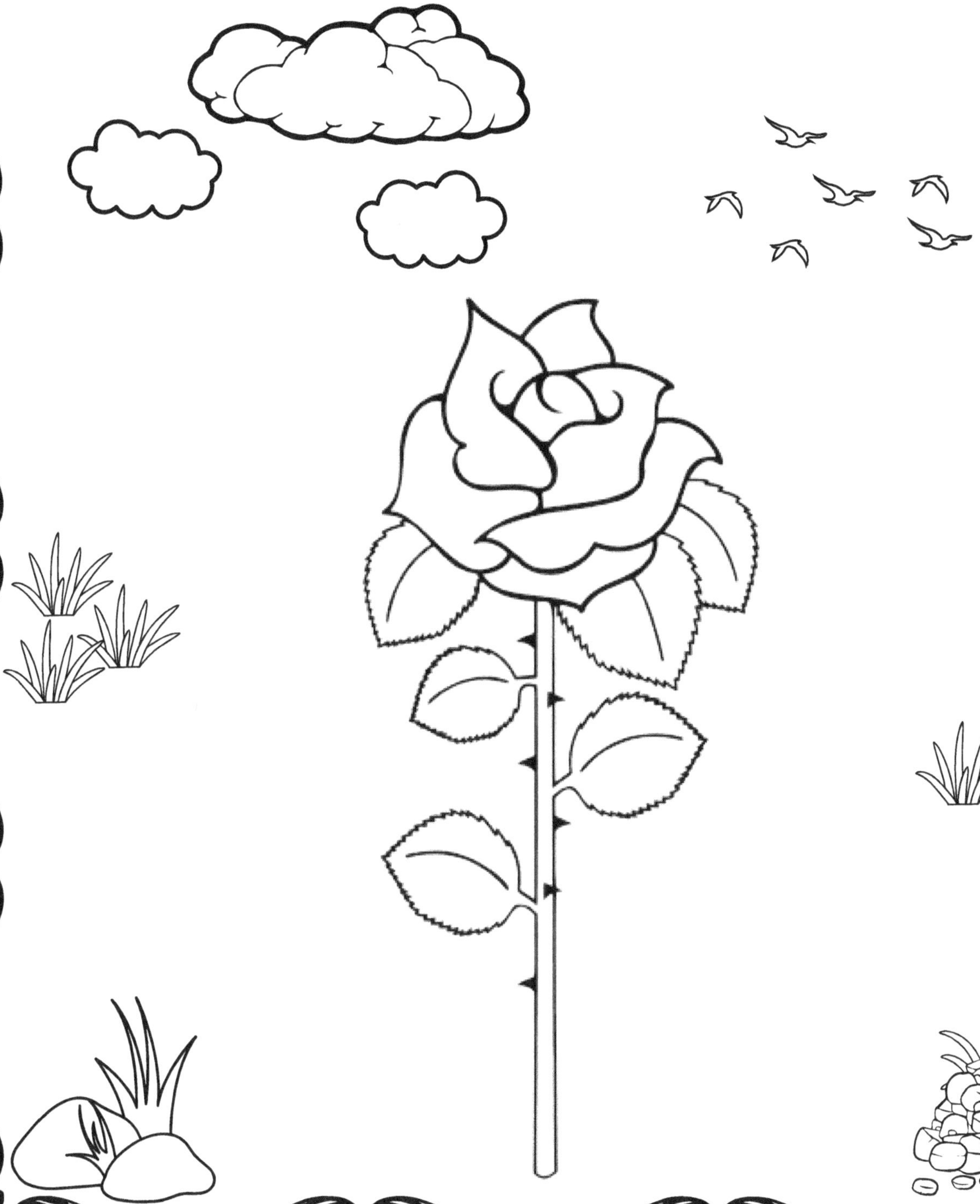

Rose Coloring Book

Rose Coloring Book

Rose Coloring Book

Rose Coloring Book

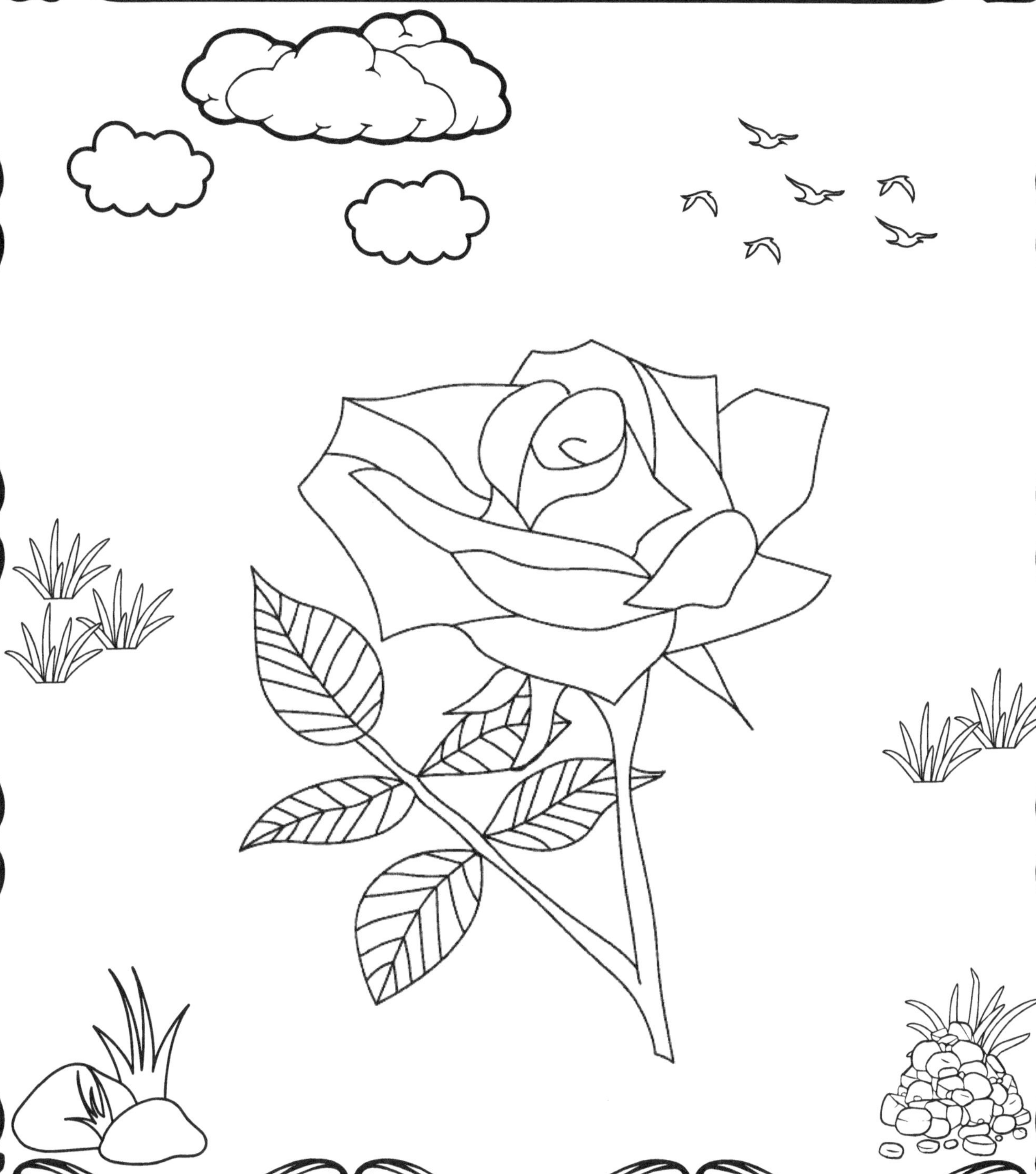

Rose Coloring Book

Rose Coloring Book

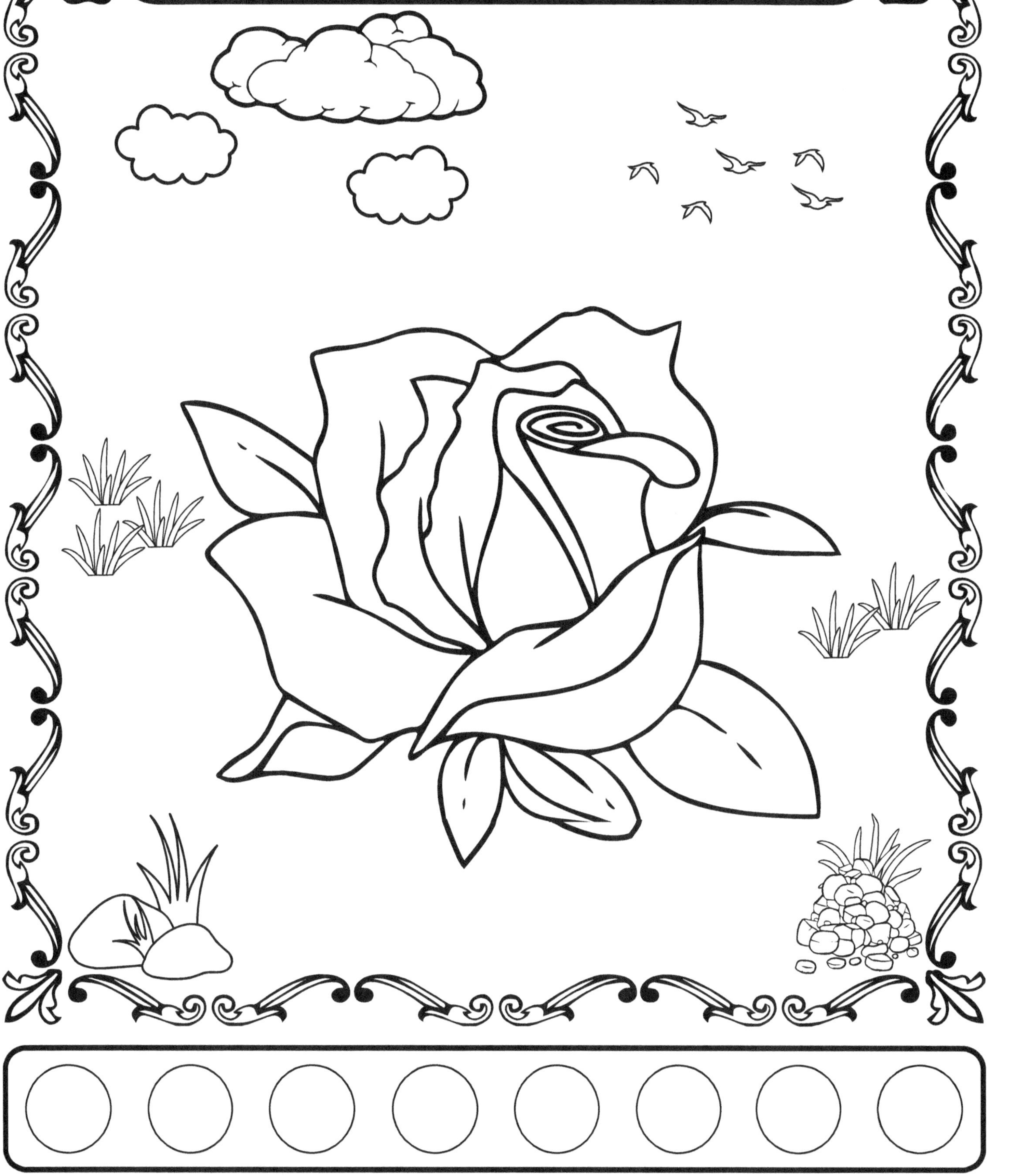

Rose Coloring Book

Rose Coloring Book

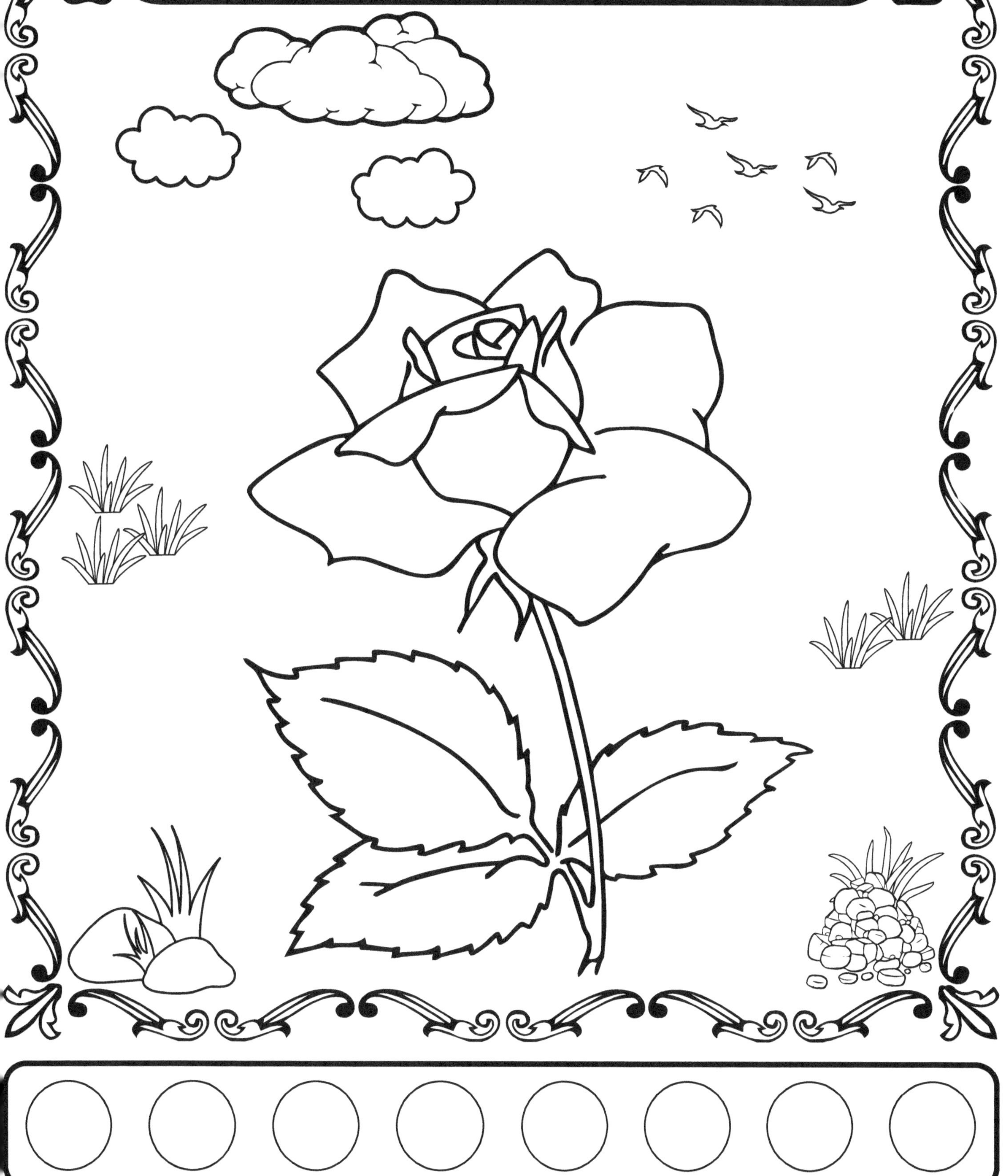

Rose Coloring Book

Rose Coloring Book

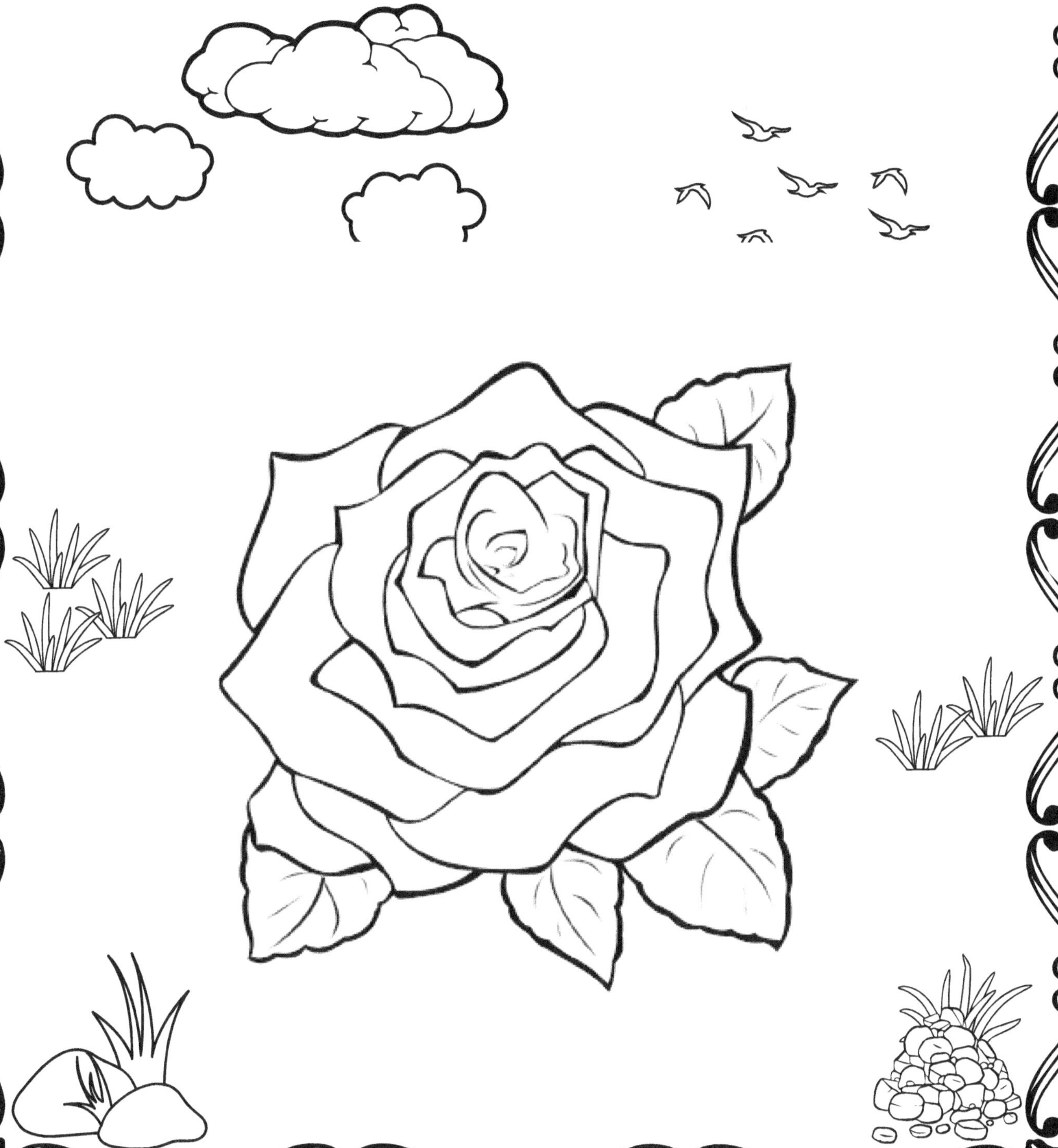

Rose Coloring Book

Rose Coloring Book

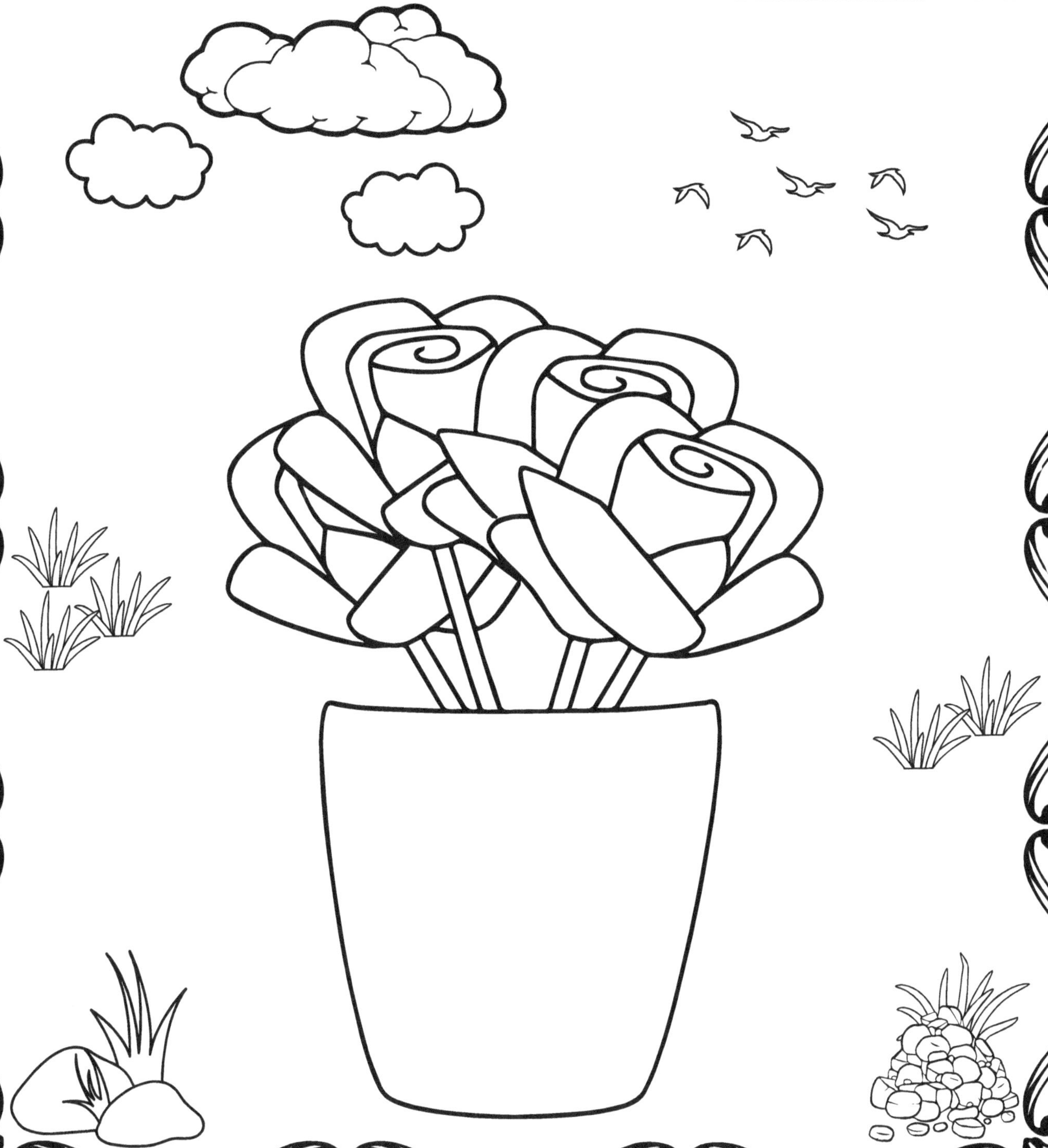

Rose Coloring Book

Rose Coloring Book

Rose Coloring Book

Rose Coloring Book

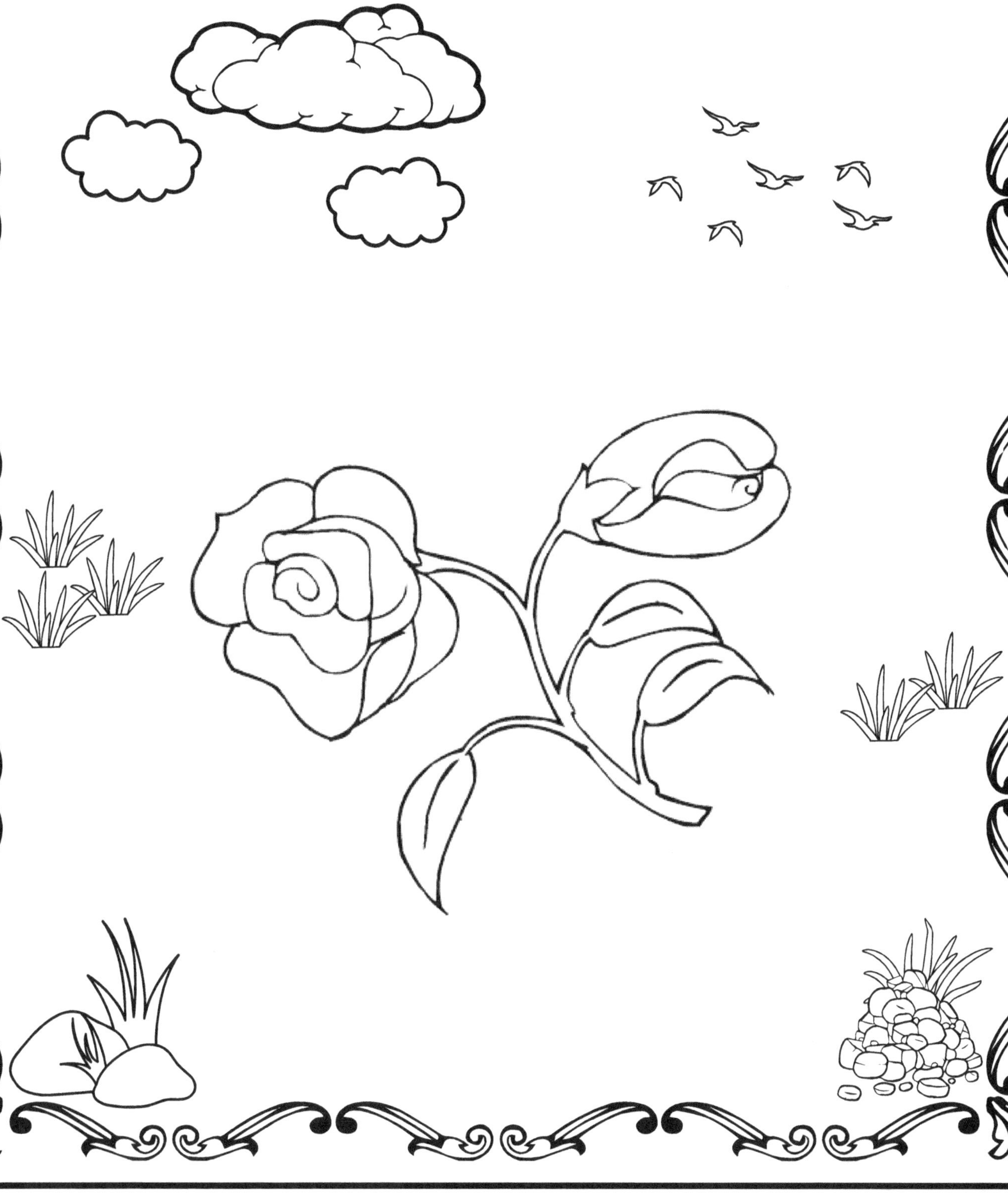

Rose Coloring Book

Rose Coloring Book

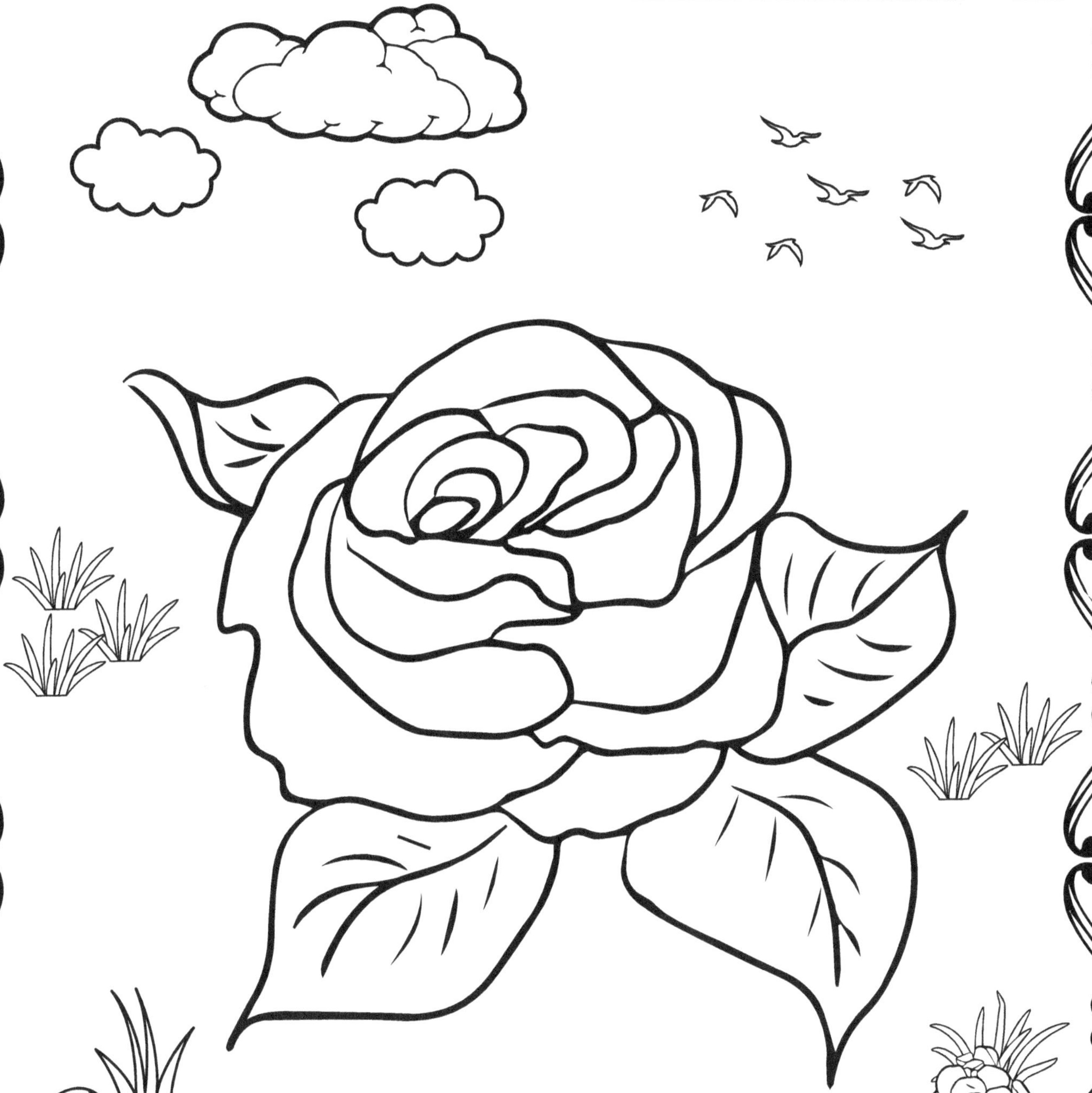

Rose Coloring Book

www.ingramcontent.com/pod-product-compliance
Lightning Source LLC
Chambersburg PA
CBHW081656220526
45466CB00009B/2779
* 9 7 9 8 5 6 4 9 0 0 0 5 8 *